ELECTRICIAN FIRST YEAR MCQ

OBJECTIVE QUESTION ANSWERS

MANOJ DOLE

Digitization is the need of the time. In the future, training in industrial training institutes will need to be conducted using online internet to make training more convenient and easy. E-books containing a set of MCQ questions will be made available to the trainees as they need to be more accustomed to the multiple choice questions MCQ to prepare for the online exams taking place in their industrial training institutes.

With all these factors in mind, Mr. Manoj Madhukar Dole Instructor, Industrial Training Institute, Satara, has written books according to the new annual system and NSQF-5 syllabus. And they've created theoretical mobile apps and blogs to make training easier, and made all these educational materials available for download on the world famous websites Google Play Store, Amazon and Apple Book Store.

The books were published by Hon'ble Joint Director Shri Rajendra Ghume Saheb Regional Office of Vocational Education and Training, Pune on 9/1/2019, at this time Shri Prakash Saigavkar Saheb Principal Government Industrial Training Institute Aundh Pune, Shri Tukaram Misal Saheb Principal Govt. Q. Sanstha Satara, Shri Sachin Dhumal Saheb District Vocational Education and Training Officer Satara, Shri Yatin Pargaonkar Saheb Principal Govt. Q. Sanstha Kolhapur, Shri Vikas Teke Saheb Inspector Vocational Education and Training Regional Office Pune, Palekar Foods Products Pvt. Ltd. Entrepreneurial Chairman of Satara Mr. Nilkanthrao Palekar Saheb, Chairman of Hira Foods Mr. Ibrahim Baba Tamboli Saheb, Mrs. Shalmali Pawar Headmaster Government Technical School Center Satara and other dignitaries were present on the occasion.

Contents

Prologue

Electrician First Year MCQ is a simple Book for ITI Engineering Course Electrician First Year, NSQF Syllabus in 2022, It contains objective questions with underlined & bold correct answers MCQ covering all topics including all about safety and environment, use of fire extinguishers, artificial respiratory resuscitation to begin with. He gets the idea of trade tools & its standardization, identifies different types of conductors, cables & their skinning & joint making. Basic electrical laws like Kirchhoff's law, ohm's law, laws of resistances and their application in different combinations of electrical circuit are practiced along with laws of magnetism. The trainee practices on circuit for single phase and poly-phase circuits for 3 wire/4 wire balanced & unbalanced loads. Skilling practice on different types & combination of cells for operation and maintenance is being done. Wiring practice with installation of different accessories like ICDP switch, distribution fuse box and mounting energy meters are practiced as per IE rules for hostel/residential building, workshop and its fault detection are done by trainee. The trainee will practice for pipe & plate earthing. Different types of light fitting are to be done like HP/LP mercury vapour and sodium vapour are prominent. The trainee will practice on different types of measuring instruments like multimeter, wattmeter, energy meter, phase sequences meter, frequency meter, for measurement of electrical parameters in single & three phase circuits. He will gain skill on range extension, calibration and testing of meters. Practice for dismantling, assembling and testing of heating element equipment, induction heating

equipment, grinding machines and washing machines will be done by trainee. Skill will be gained on transformer for operation, efficiency, series parallel operation, replacement of transformer oil and combination of single-phase transformers for 3 phase operation. The trainee will practice on winding of small transformer, and lots more.

We add new question answers with each new version. Please email us in case of any errors/omissions. This is arguably the largest and best Book for All engineering multiple choice questions and answers.

As a student you can use it for your exam prep. This e-Book is also useful for professors to refresh material.

Foreword

Vocational education and training is imparted through the Department of Vocational Education and Training through the Department of Business Education and Business Practical to supply multi-skilled artisans in line with the rapidly growing demand in the industrial sector in the 21st century. All the occupations within the institutions are important, as the trainees from these occupations develop multi-skills as per the demands of the industry.

with the noble intention of making available MCQ e-books suitable for all businesses, considering that all the examinations in all the industries in the industrial sector are conducted online and include MCQ method questions. Mr. Manoj Madhukar Dole has written a very good e-book on MCQ method as per the new annual syllabus. This e-book will definitely be a guide for all the trainees, trainee candidates, training instructors and others concerned.

The author of the book is Mr. Manoj Madhukar Dole, Instructor Gov. ITI Satara has 17 years of training experience. Written as a new annual pattern, this e-book incorporates modern digital QR Code technology to understand the layout, simple language, and simple syntax, diagrams and videos for each subject. So I am sure that this e-book will definitely be useful for in-depth study and exam practice. The work they have done is certainly commendable.

Mr. Tukaram Misal
Principal Government Industrial Training Institute Satara.

Preface

DGET New Delhi and CSTARI Kolkata have been implementing an annual pattern for all businesses in ITI since the August 2018 session. The examination system will also be changed and it will be online from this year and since all the questions are of Objective Type (MCQ), the trainees are in dire need of in-depth study. It is with this in mind that we are delighted to present the books based on the old NIMI pattern and a complete overview of the new annual pattern, and we hope that these books will be a guide for all business directors and trainees. Is.

For writing these books, Johar Awate Saheb, Principal of ITI Akluj. Former Principal of ITI Satara Saigavkar Saheb, Assistant Director Shri Chandrakant Dhekne Saheb Regional Office of Vocational Education and Training, Pune, District Vocational Education and Training Officer Sachin Dhumal Saheb and Headmaster Government Technical School Kendra Shalmali Pawar Madam and son Adhiraj Dole, mother Kusum Dole, I am very grateful to my father Madhukar Dole and wife Ashwini Dole for their special guidance and cooperation from time to time.

Also, in a very short period of time, the book was reviewed by Shri Rajendra Ghume Saheb, Joint Director, Vocational Education and Training Regional Office, Pune, for his invaluable time in publishing the book. I am sincerely grateful for their feedback.

I am grateful to the Instructor of ITI Satara for there continuous support from the very beginning of writing the book.

From this book, I consider myself blessed to have shared my thoughts on e-learning with you. I will not claim that this book is perfect, because considering the perfection, this book is an attempt and is in its infancy. They will be valuable for improvement if they are tested and suggested.

Manoj Dole
Dated 9/1/2019

Acknowledgements

The industrial training and theoretical examination system of our industrial training institutes and these changes have been accepted by the craft instructors and the trainees. Theoretical examinations conducted in your industrial training institutes are also conducted online. Since these examinations are of multiple choice MCQ method, the trainees will need to get more practice of such questions.

With all these considerations in mind, Mr. Manoj Madhukar, Director, Dole Crafts, Katari Industrial Training Institute, Satara, has done a thorough study and with his diligent work and added his keen intellect, according to the new annual system and NSQF-5 syllabus, e-book of Katari and other machine trades. -Book) and they have created mobile apps and blogs on theoretical topics to make training easier and have made all these educational materials available for download on the world famous websites Google Play Store, Amazon and Apple Book Store. Training has been made easier by creating a print version and using advanced techniques like QR Code.

All these educational materials will definitely be a guide for all the trainees for in-depth study and for the craft instructors and other concerned who are imparting vocational training.

CHAPTER ONE

Electrician First Year QR Code Images fr e-Learning

Download App
Online Test Exam
ITI Books
AutoCAD CAM
JOB & Apprentice
Online Theory
Computer Course
Trading Course
CNC Course
MSCIT Course
Shopping Business
Internet Business
Web Designing
Online Services
Top Sportsmans
Indian Army
Freedom Fighters
Top Scientists
Social Reformers
Motivational Speaker
Top Richest People
Join WhatsApp Group
Join Facebook Group
Like Facebook Page
PAN / Adhar / Licence
Passport

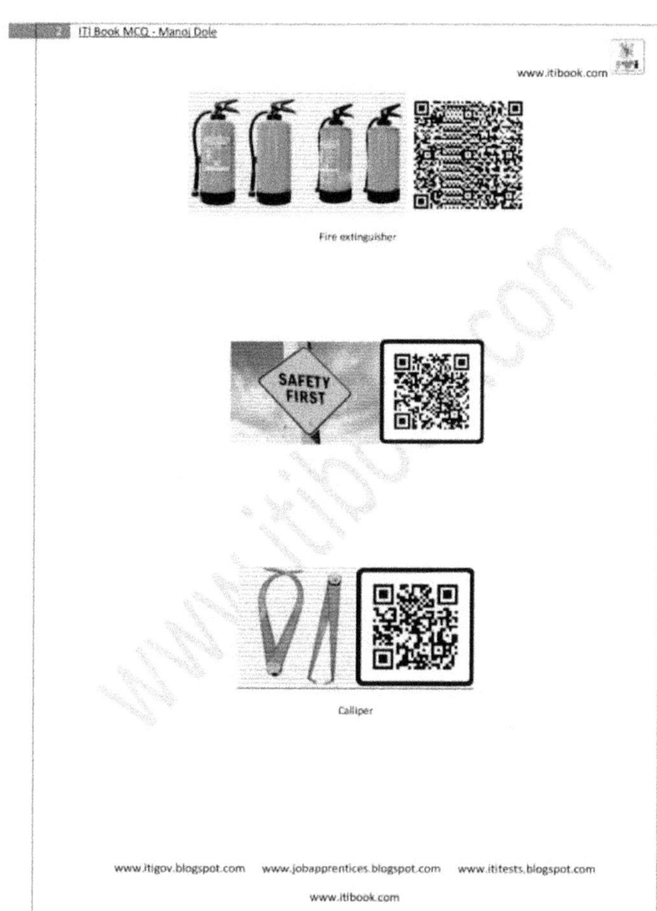
2 ITI Book MCQ - Manoj Dole
www.itibook.com
SAFETY FIRST
www.itigov.blogspot.com www.jobapprentices.blogspot.com www.ititests.blogspot.com
www.itibook.com

5 ITI Book MCQ - Manoj Dole
www.itibook.com
Hacksaw frame
Universal surface guage
Hammer
www.itigov.blogspot.com www.jobapprentices.blogspot.com www.ititests.blogspot.com
www.itibook.com

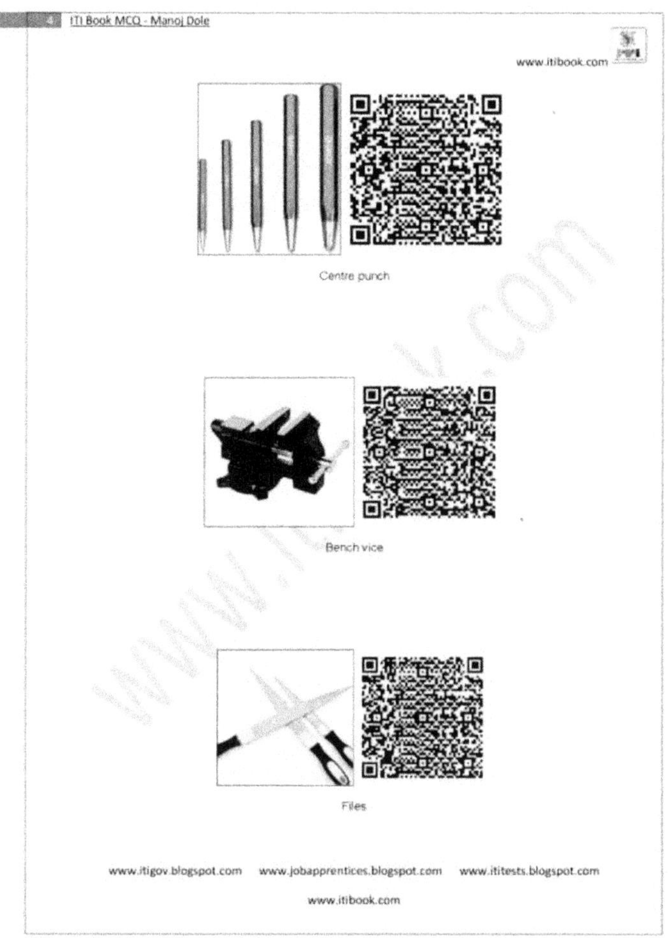
4 ITI Book MCQ - Manoj Dole
www.itibook.com
Centre punch
Bench vice
Files
www.itigov.blogspot.com www.jobapprentices.blogspot.com www.ititests.blogspot.com
www.itibook.com

7 ITI Book MCQ - Manoj Dole
www.itibook.com
Vernier bevel protractor
www.itigov.blogspot.com www.jobapprentices.blogspot.com www.ititests.blogspot.com
www.itibook.com

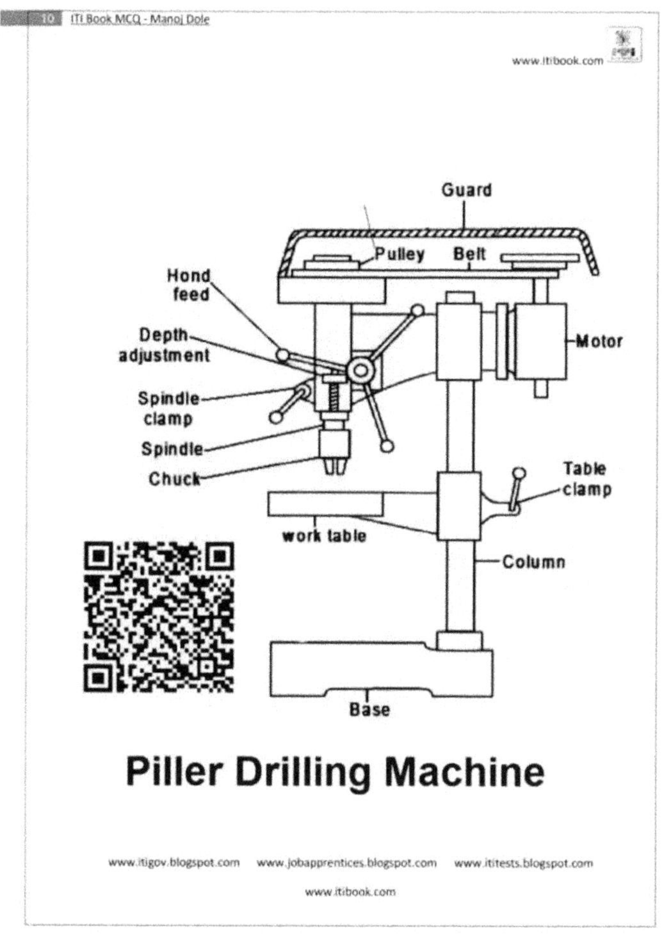
10 ITI Book MCQ - Manoj Dole
www.itibook.com
Guard
Pulley
Belt
Hond feed
Depth adjustment
Motor
Spindle clamp
Spindle
Chuck
Table clamp
work table
Column
Base
Piller Drilling Machine
www.itigov.blogspot.com www.jobapprentices.blogspot.com www.ititests.blogspot.com
www.itibook.com

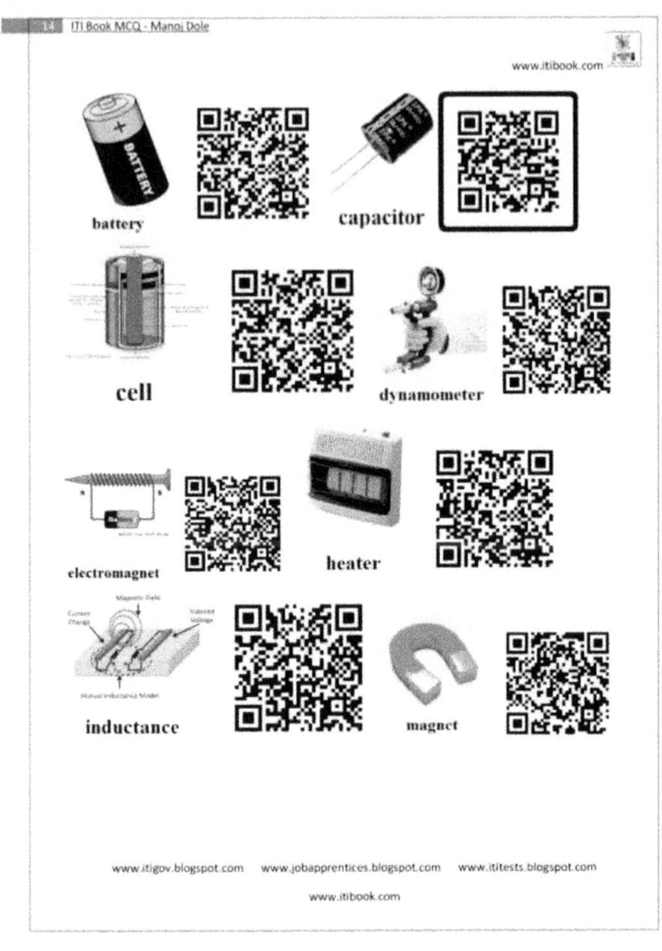
14 ITI Book MCQ - Manoj Dole
www.itibook.com
battery
capacitor
cell
dynamometer
electromagnet
heater
inductance
magnet
www.itigov.blogspot.com www.jobapprentices.blogspot.com www.ititests.blogspot.com
www.itibook.com

15 ITi Book MCQ - Manoj Dole
www.itibook.com
megger
motor
multimeter
ohmmeter
resistores
star connected
alternator
voltmeter
ammeter
wattmeter
www.itigov.blogspot.com www.jobapprentices.blogspot.com www.ititests.blogspot.com
www.itibook.com

Coffee maker
Blender
Mixer
Toaster
Microwave
Crock pot
Rice cooker
Pressure cooker
Bachelor griller (U.K.)
Stove
Lamp
Light bulb
Lantern
Torch
Clothes iron
Electric drill

Kettle
Water cooker (UK)
/Electric kettle
/Hot pot (US)
Water
purifier
Vacuum
cleaner
Electric
fan
Evaporative
cooler
Air
conditioner
Television
Speaker
Clothes
dryer

CHAPTER TWO

Electrician First Year MCQ

01] In case of bleeding, take treatment Of

D] cold 3" and rest

<u>A] spray cold water</u>

B] Bandage immediately -----

B] Enquire about the accident thought treatment

02] in case of an accident, the victim should im

A] Asked to take rest

<u>C] Attended immediately</u>

D] leave him

03] First aid is given to an injured or ill person primarily

A] Save life

B] Prevent further deterioration of the muff's

C] Give best possible comfort

<u>D] All of these</u>

04] Colour code for Bins for waste paper segregation is -----

<u>A] blue Colour</u>

B] Yellow Colour

C] Red Colour

D] Green Colour

05] In Japanese Seiko stands for -------------

<u>A] Shine</u>

B] Sort

C] Standardize

D] Sustain

06] Benefit of SS system is ------

A] Increase in productivity

B] Increase in quality

C] Reduction in wastage of time

D] All of these

07] Safety is -----------

A] nobody's business

B] every bodise business

C] Some bodies business

D] The organization business

08] For basic categories of safety signs are available The meaning of"prohibition" sign ----

A] shows it must not be done

B] Shows what must be done

C] Warns the hazard or danger

D] Gives information of safety provision

09] Which one is a workshop safety?

A] Keep shop floor clean and free from grease, oil or other slippery materials

B] Stop the machine before changing the speed

C] Don't use cracked or chipped tools

D] Don't try to stop a running machine with hand

10] In Personal Protect Equipment (PPE] HELMET is used to

A] protect head

B] Protect eyes

C] Protect hands

D] Protect ears

11] Which of the following belongs to general safety?

A Have a worker in good attitude

B] The work clean and clear

C] Concentrate on your work

D] Keep the floor and gangways clean and clear

12] While grinding, which is used to protect the eyes?

A] Dark green glass

B] Mask

C] Sun glasses

D] Safety goggles

13] Which of the following is done for machine safety?

A] Check the oil level before starting the machine

B] Do things in a methodical way

C] Keep the floor and gangways clean and clear

D] Don't use dies and scarves

14] ln Personal Protect Equipment (PPE], 'sleeves' is used to protect ----------

A] Face

B] Eyes

C] Ears

D] Hands

15] ABC stands for --------------

A] Automatic Breathing Control

B] Automatic Blood Control

C] Airway Breathing Circulation

D] Automatic Blood Circulation

04] Fire & FIRE EXTINGUISHERS

16] To put off"Class B" fire, the types of fire extinguisher used is

A] dry power

B] Carbon dioxide

C] Jet of water

D] Foam type

17] Which type of fire extinguisher is used to put off general fire?

A] Water type Extinguisher

B] Foam type Extinguisher

C] Dry chemical powder Extinguisher

D] Carbon dioxide (C02] Extinguisher

18] One micrometer (U] is equal to

A] 01mm

B] 001mm

C] 0001mm

D] 00001mm

19] The caliper meant for measuring the width of a slot is

A] Odd leg caliper

B] Outside caliper

C] Jenny caliper

D] Inside calliper

20] The size of the dividers are specified by the -----------

A] Total length of legs

B] Distance between the points when fully opened

C] Length of legs without points

D] distance between the pivot and the point

21] The instrument used to mark parallel lines, parallel to the datum edge is -

A] jenny caliper

B] Divider

C] Outside calliper

D] Inside calliper

22] Which one of the following is an indirect measuring tool?

A] Outside caliper

B] Vernier calliper

C] Steel rule

D] Outside micrometer

23] For cutting thin tubing, the most suitable pitch of the hacksaw blade is

A] 18mm

B] 14mm

C] 1mm

D] 08mm

24] For cutting solid brass, the most suitable pitch of the hacksaw blade is

A] 18mm

B] 14mm

C] 1mm

D] 08mm

25] A new hacksaw blade after a few strokes becomes loose because of the

A] Stretching of the blade

B] Wing-nut threads being worn out

C] Wrong pitch of the blade

D] Improper selection of the set of saws

26] While cutting small diameter pipes, it is advisable to watch regularly and ensure that

A] The cut is along the curved line

B] More saw teeth are in contract

C] The work is not overheated

D] Proper balancing of hacksaw is maintained

27] The vice clamps are used to

A] Protect hard jaws

B] Clamp the work pieces rigidly

C] Protect the finished surfaces

D] Prevent the movable jaw being filed

28] The reference surface during marking is provided by the

A] Surface gauge

B] Workpiece

C] Drawing of the work

D] Marking table surface

29] The size of an engineer's vice is specified by the

A] Length of the movable jaw

B] Width of the jaws

C] Height of the vice

D] Maximum opening of the jaws

30] The part of the universal surface gauge which helps to draw a parallel line along a datum edge is the

A] Rocker arm

B] Snug

C] Fine adjustment screw

D] Guide pins

31] Scribers are made of

A] Mild steel

B] High carbon steel

C] Brass

D] Cast iron

32] Portion of the hammer used for fixing the handle is

A] Face

B] Peen

C] Cheek

D] Eye hole

33] Weight of the hammer for the marking purpose is

A] 250g

B] 500g

C] 1 kg

D] 2 kgs

34] The size of the dividers are specified by the

A] Total length of the legs

B] Distance between the points when fully opened

C] Length of legs without the points

D] Distance between the pivot and the point

35] The included angle of the groove of 'V' block is always

A] 45◦

B] 60◦

C] 90◦

D] 120◦

36] 'V' blocks are available in grades of

A] A & B

B] A,B & C

C] 1,2 & 3

D] 1 & 2

37] 'V' blocks of grade 'B' are made of

A] Cast iron

B] Mild steel

C] Steel

D] Cast steel

38] Name the punch used to locate the centre

A] Prick punch 30°

B] Prick punch 60°

C] Centre punch

D] Dot punch

39] The point angle of centre punch is --------

A] 30°

B] 50°

c] 900

D] 1200

40] Punches are used for forming ---------of any shape

A] Holes

B] Mining

C] Knurling

D] Reaming

41] Generally the length of the handle of the vice is ----------

A] 15 times the normal size of the vice

B] 25 times the normal size of the vice

C] 35 times the normal size of the vice

D] 45 times the normal size of the vice

42] Bench vice spindle is made of

A] mild steel

B] Cast iron

C] Tool steel
D] Bronze
43] The convexity of files helps
A] To file concave surfaces
B] To file convex surfaces
C] To prevent rounding of edges of work
D] The file to become straight when pressure is applied
44] Which file used for filling wood, leather and other soft material?
A] Single cut file
B] Double cut file
c] Rasp cut file
D] Curved cut file
45] File used is used for ------------
A] Cleaning the work piece
C] Renewing the file teeth
B] cleaning the file teeth
D] Cleaning the chips
46] File card is used to --------
A] Clean the work piece
C] Renew the file teeth
B] Clean the file teeth
47] The point angle of scriber is -----------
A] 30°
B] 60°
C] 5° to 10°
D] 12° to 15°
48] The cutting angle for chipping cast iron is
A] 375°
B] 55°
C] 60°
D] 90°
49] The chisel will dig into the material when
A] The rake angle is more
B] The clearance angle is too low
C] The angle of inclination is more
D] The angle of inclination is too low
50] A slight convexity is given to the cutting edge to
A] Cut curved surfaces

B] Cut sharp corners

C] Prevent digging of the ends

D] Allow the lubricant to enter

51] Surface plates are made of

A] High grade cast steel

B] Fine-grained cast iron

C] Alloy steels

D] Wrought iron

52] The taper shank drills are held on the machine by means of

A] Chucks

B] Sleeves

C] Drift

D] Vice

53] Drill chucks are fitted on the drilling machine spindle by means of a

A] Knurled ring

B] Arbor

C] Drift

D] Pinion and key

54] The Morse taper provided on drills ranges between

A] MT 1 to MT 5

B] MT 1 to MT 4

C] MT 0 to MT 5

D] MT 0 to MT 4

55] A drift is used for

A] Drawing a drill location

B] Fixing chuck on the machine spindle

C] Removing a broken drill from the work

D] Removing the drill from the machine spindle

56] When the taper shank of the drill is larger than the machine spindle, the device to hold the drill is a

A] Drill sleeve

B] Taper socket

C] Drill drift

D] Chuck and key

57] The suitable cutting fluid for drilling mild steel in a drilling machine is

A] Synthetic soluble oil

B] Neat oil

C] Distilled water

D] Soluble oil

58] A special feature of the radial drilling machine is

A] It can be used for drilling with a HSS drill

B] Table can be moved and set at any position

C] A variety of speeds is available

D] The spindle can be brought to any position

59] The point angle of drills depends on

A] The size of the drill

B] The type of machine

C] The material of the work

D] The RPM of the drill

60] The point angle for a standard drill is

A] 60◦

B] 108◦

C] 118◦

D] 135◦

61] The helical angle determines the

A] Cutting angle

B] Chew angle

C] Rake angle

D] Lip angle

62] The clearance angle of the drill is between

A] 3◦ to 5◦

B] 8◦ to 12◦

C] 12◦ to 20◦

D] 15◦ to 20◦

63] In a remote place (no electricity available] a rail track is to be drilled Choose the right drilling machine

A] Radial drilling machine

B] Pillar drilling machine

C] Ratchet drilling machine

D] Sensitive drilling Machine

64] A drilling machine used by a carpenter for cabinet making is a

A] Ratchet drilling machine

B] Radial drilling machine

C] Breast drilling machine

D] Sensitive drilling machine

65] Which one of the following drilling machines is used for drilling holes where electricity is not available?

A] Bench drilling machine

B] Pillar drilling machine

C] Redial drilling machine

D] Ratchet drilling machine

66] Which one of the following drilling machine is used for heavy duty work?

A] Bench drilling machine

B] Pillar drilling machine

C] Radial drilling machine

D] Electric hand drilling machine

67] Drill chuck are held on the machine spindle by means of ------

A] arbor

B] Drift

C] draw-in bar

D] Chuck nut

68] Different speeds are obtained in a sensitive bench drilling machine by ----

A] Belt pulley mechanism

B] Hydraulic mechanism

C] Rack and Pinion mechanism

D] Cam and follower mechanism

69] Tap are re sharpened by grinding -----

A] Hutes

B] Threads

C] Diameter

D] Relief

70] The tapping drill size for M10 x 15 is ----------

A] 82

B] 83

C] 84

D] 85

71] A nut is to be made for a screw of M10XIS What should be the size of drilled hole?

A] 8-5 mm

B] 90 mm

C] 95 mm

D] 100 mm

72] Ribs are given on the unmachined portion of the angle plate for

A] Easy handling

B] Convenience in manufacturing

C] Clamping while setting on machines

D] Rigidity and to prevent distortion

73] The slots on the angle plate are given for

A] Reducing weight

B] Aligning the work

C] Lifting using hooks

D] Accommodating bolts

74] The size of the angle plates is stated by

A] Weight

B] Length

C] Length x width

D] Size number

75] for making gutters, roof flashing, hoods etc

A] Galvanised iron

B] Stainless steel

C] Copper sheet

D] Metal sheets

76] in dairies food processing, kitchen ware etc

A] Galvanised iron

B] Stainless steel

C] Copper sheet

D] Metal sheets

77] for making buckets, heating ducts, cabinets etc

A] Galvanised iron

B] Stainless steel

C] Copper sheet

D] Metal sheets

78] in canneries and chemical plants Metal sheets

A] Galvanised iron

B] Stainless steel

C] Copper sheet

D] Metal sheets

79] Rivets for Joining sheets to thick plates]

A] Countersunk head
B] Flat head
C] Pan head
D] Mushroom
80] Rivets for Joining sheet metal]
A] Countersunk head
B] Flat head
C] Pan head
D] Mushroom
81] Rivets for Heavy fabrication work]
A] Countersunk head
B] Flat head
C] Pan head
D] Mushroom
82] Rivets for Reduces the height of rivet head above the meta\ surface
A] Countersunk head
B] Flat head
C] Pan head
D] Mushroom
83] Rivets for commonly used for structural work]
A] Countersunk head
B] Flat head
C] Pan head
D] Snap head
84] Which one of the following fire extinguisher is suitable for a live electrical fire?
A] halon
B] water
C] foam
D] liquefied chemical
1. The S.I. unit of power is
(a) Henry
(b) coulomb
(c) watt
(d) watt-hour
2. Electric pressure is also called
(a) resistance
(b) power

(c) voltage
(d) energy
3. The substances which have a large number of free electrons and offer a low
resistance are called
(a) insulators
(b) inductors
(c) semi-conductors
(d) conductors
4. Out of the following which is not a poor conductor ?
(a) Cast iron
(b) Copper
(c) Carbon
(d) Tungsten
5. Out of the following which is an insulating material ?
(a) Copper
(b) Gold
(c) Silver
(d) Paper
6. The property of a conductor due to which it passes current is called
(a) resistance
(b) reluctance
(c) conductance
(d) inductance
7. Conductance is reciprocal of
(a) resistance
(b) inductance
(c) reluctance
(d) capacitance
8. The resistance of a conductor varies inversely as
(a) length
(b) area of cross-section
(c) temperature
(d) resistivity
9. With rise in temperature the resistance of pure metals
(a) increases
(b) decreases
(c) first increases and then decreases

(d) remains constant

10. With rise in temperature the resistance of semi-conductors

(a) decreases

(b) increases

(c) first increases and then decreases

(d) remains constant

11. The resistance of a copper wire 200 m long is 21 Q. If its thickness (diameter)

is 0.44 mm, its specific resistance is around

(a) 1.2 x 10~8 Q-m

(b) 1.4 x 10~8 Q-m

(c) 1.6 x 10""8 Q-m

(d) 1.8 x 10"8 Q-m

13. An instrument which detects electric current is known as

(a) voltmeter

(b) rheostat

(c) wattmeter

(d) galvanometer

14. In a circuit a 33 Q resistor carries a current of 2 A. The voltage across the resistor is

(a) 33 V

(b) 66 v

(c) 80 V

(d) 132 V

15. A light bulb draws 300 mA when the voltage across it is 240 V. The resistance of the light bulb is

(a) 400 Q

(b) 600 Q

(c) 800 Q

(d) 1000 Q

16. The resistance of a parallel circuit consisting of two branches is 12 ohms. If the resistance of one branch is 18 ohms, what is the resistance of the other ?

(a) 18 Q

(b) 36 Q

(c) 48 Q

(d) 64 Q

17. Four wires of same material, the same cross-sectional area and the same length when connected in parallel give a resistance of 0.25 Q. If the same four wires are connected is series the effective resistance will be

(a) 1 Q

(b) 2 Q

(c) 3 Q

(d) 4 Q

18. A current of 16 amperes divides between two branches in parallel of resistances 8 ohms and 12 ohms respectively. The current in each branch is

(a) 6.4 A, 6.9 A

(b) 6.4 A, 9.6 A

(c) 4.6 A, 6.9 A

(d) 4.6 A, 9.6 A

19. Current velocity through a copper conductor is

(a) the same as propagation velocity of electric energy

(b) independent of current strength

(c) of the order of a few ^.s/m

(d) nearly 3 x 108 m/s

20. Which of the following material has nearly zero temperature co-efficient of resistance?

(a) Manganin

(b) Porcelain

(c) Carbon

(d) Copper

21. You have to replace 1500 Q resistor in radio. You have no 1500 Q resistor but have several 1000 Q ones which you would connect

(a) two in parallel

(b) two in parallel and one in series

(c) three in parallel

(d) three in series

22. Two resistors are said to be connected in series when

(a) same current passes in turn through both

(b) both carry the same value of current

(c) total current equals the sum of branch currents

(d) sum of IR drops equals the applied e.m.f.

23. Which of the following statement is true both for a series and a parallel D.C. circuit?

(a) Elements have individual currents

(b) Currents are additive

(c) Voltages are additive

(d) Power are additive

24. Which of the following materials has a negative temperature co-efficient of resistance?

(a) Copper

(b) Aluminum

(c) Carbon

(d) Brass

25. Ohm's law is not applicable to

(a) vacuum tubes

(b) carbon resistors

(c) high voltage circuits

(d) circuits with low current densities

26. Which is the best conductor of electricity ?

(a) Iron

(b) Silver

(c) Copper

(d) Carbon

27. For which of the following 'ampere second' could be the unit ?

(a) Reluctance

(b) Charge

(c) Power

(d) Energy

28. All of the following are equivalent to watt except

(a) (amperes) ohm

(b) joules/sec.

(c) amperes x volts

(d) amperes/volt

29. A resistance having rating 10 ohms, 10 W is likely to be a

(a) metallic resistor

(b) carbon resistor

(c) wire wound resistor

(d) variable resistor

30. Which one of the following does not have negative temperature co-efficient ?

(a) Aluminium

(b) Paper

(c) Rubber
(d) Mica
31. Varistors are
(a) insulators
(6) non-linear resistors
(c) carbon resistors
(d) resistors with zero temperature coefficient
32. Insulating materials have the function of
(a) preventing a short circuit between conducting wires
(b) preventing an open circuit between the voltage source and the load
(c) conducting very large currents
(d) storing very high currents
33. The rating of a fuse wire is always expressed in
(a) ampere-hours
(b) ampere-volts
(c) kWh
(d) amperes
34. The minimum charge on an ion is
(a) equal to the atomic number of the atom
(b) equal to the charge of an electron
(c) equal to the charge of the number of electrons in an atom (#) zero
35. In a series circuit with unequal resistances
(a) the highest resistance has the most of the current through it
(b) the lowest resistance has the highest voltage drop
(c) the lowest resistance has the highest current
(d) the highest resistance has the highest voltage drop
36. The filament of an electric bulb is made of
(a) carbon
(b) aluminium
(c) tungsten
(d) nickel
37. A 3 Q resistor having 2 A current will dissipate the power of
(a) 2 watts
(b) 4 watts
(c) 6 watts
(d) 8 watts
38. Which of the following statement is true?
(a) A galvanometer with low resistance in parallel is a voltmeter

(b) A galvanometer with high resistance in parallel is a voltmeter

(c) A galvanometer resistance in series is an ammeter with low

(d) A galvanometer with high resistance in series is an ammeter

39. The resistance of a few meters of wire conductor in closed electrical circuit is

(a) practically zero

(b) low

(c) high

(d) very high

40. If a parallel circuit is opened in the main line, the current

(a) increases in the branch of the lowest resistance

(b) increases in each branch

(c) is zero in all branches

(d) is zero in the highest resistive branch

41. If a wire conductor of 0.2 ohm resistance is doubled in length, its resistance becomes

(a) 0.4 ohm

(b) 0.6 ohm

(c) 0.8 ohm

(d) 1.0 ohm

42. Three 60 W bulbs are in parallel across the 60 V power line. If one bulb burns open

(a) there will be heavy current in the main line

(b) rest of the two bulbs will not light

(c) all three bulbs will light

(d) the other two bulbs will light

43. The four bulbs of 40 W each are connected in series swift a battery across them, which of the following statement is true ?

(a) The current through each bulb in same

(b) The voltage across each bulb is not same

(c) The power dissipation in each bulb is not same

(d) None of the above

44. Two resistances Rl and Ri are connected in series across the voltage source where Rl>Ri. The largest drop will be across

(a) Rl

(b) Ri

(c) either Rl or Ri

(d) none of them

46. A closed switch has a resistance of

(a) zero

(b) about 50 ohms

(c) about 500 ohms

(d) infinity

47. The hot resistance of the bulb's filament is higher than its cold resistance because the temperature co-efficient of the filament is

(a) zero

(b) negative

(c) positive

(d) about 2 ohms per degree

49. The insulation on a current carrying conductor is provided

(a) to prevent leakage of current

(b) to prevent shock

(c) both of above factors

(d) none of above factors

50. The thickness of insulation provided on the conductor depends on

(a) the magnitude of voltage on the conductor

(b) the magnitude of current flowing through it

(c) both (a) and (b)

(d) none of the above

51. Which of the following quantities remain the same in all parts of a series circuit ?

(a) Voltage

(b) Current

(c) Power

(d) Resistance

52. A 40 W bulb is connected in series with a room heater. If now 40 W bulb is replaced by 100 W bulb, the heater output will

(a) decrease

(b) increase

(c) remain same

(d) heater will burn out

53. In an electric kettle water boils in 10 m minutes. It is required to boil the boiler in 15 minutes, using same supply mains

(a) length of heating element should be decreased

(b) length of heating element should be increased

(c) length of heating element has no effect on heating if water

(d) none of the above

54. An electric filament bulb can be worked from

(a) D.C. supply only

(b) A.C. supply only

(c) Battery supply only

(d) All above

55. Resistance of a tungsten lamp as applied voltage increases

(a) decreases

(b) increases

(c) remains same

(d) none of the above

56. Electric current passing through the circuit produces

(a) magnetic effect

(b) luminous effect

(c) thermal effect

(d) chemical effect

(e) all above effects

57. Resistance of a material always decreases if

(a) temperature of material is decreased

(6) temperature of material is increased

(c) number of free electrons available become more

(d) none of the above is correct

58. If the efficiency of a machine is to be high, what should be low ?

(a) Input power

(b) Losses

(c) True component of power

(d) kWh consumed

(e) Ratio of output to input

59. When electric current passes through a metallic conductor, its temperature rises. This is due to

(a) collisions between conduction electrons and atoms

(b) the release of conduction electrons from parent atoms

(c) mutual collisions between metal atoms

(d) mutual collisions between conducting electrons

60. Two bulbs of 500 W and 200 W rated at 250 V will have resistance ratio as

(a) 4 : 25

(b) 25 : 4

(c) 2 : 5

(d) 5 : 2

61. A glass rod when rubbed with silk cloth is charged because

(a) it takes in proton

(b) its atoms are removed

(c) it gives away electrons

(d) it gives away positive charge

62. Whether circuit may be AC. or D.C. one, following is most effective in

reducing the magnitude of the current.

(a) Reactor

(b) Capacitor

(c) Inductor

(d) Resistor

63. It becomes more difficult to remove

(a) any electron from the orbit

(6) first electron from the orbit

(c) second electron from the orbit

(d) third electron from the orbit

64. When one leg of parallel circuit is opened out the total current will

(a) reduce

(b) increase

(c) decrease

(d) become zero

65. In a lamp load when more than one lamp are switched on the total resistance

of the load

(a) increases

(b) decreases

(c) remains same

(d) none of the above

66. Two lamps 100 W and 40 W are connected in series across 230 V (alternating).

Which of the following statement is correct ?

(a) 100 W lamp will glow brighter

(b) 40 W lamp will glow brighter

(c) Both lamps will glow equally bright

(d) 40 W lamp will fuse

67. Resistance of 220 V, 100 W lamp will be

(a) 4.84 Q

(b) 48.4 Q

(c) 484 ft

(d) 4840 Q

68. In the case of direct current

(a) magnitude and direction of current remains constant

(b) magnitude and direction of current changes with time

(c) magnitude of current changes with time

(d) magnitude of current remains constant

69. When electric current passes through a bucket full of water, lot of bubbling is

observed. This suggests that the type of supply is

(a) A.C.

(b) D.C.

(c) any of above two

(d) none of the above

70. Resistance of carbon filament lamp as the applied voltage increases.

(a) increases

(b) decreases

(c) remains same

(d) none of the above

71. Bulbs in street lighting are all connected in

(a) parallel

(b) series

(c) series-parallel

(d) end-to-end

72. For testing appliances, the wattage of test lamp should be

(a) very low

(b) low

(c) high

(d) any value

73. Switching of a lamp in house produces noise in the radio. This is because switching operation produces

(a) arcs across separating contacts

(b) mechanical noise of high intensity

(c) both mechanical noise and arc between contacts

(d) none of the above

74. Sparking occurs when a load is switched off because the circuit has high

(a) resistance

(b) inductance

(c) capacitance

(d) impedance

75. Copper wire of certain length and resistance is drawn out to three times its

length without change in volume, the new resistance of wire becomes

(a) 1/9 times

(b) 3 times

(c) 9 times

(d) unchanged

76. When resistance element of a heater fuses and then we reconnect it after removing a portion of it, the power of the heater will

(a) decrease

(b) increase

(c) remain constant

(d) none of the above

77. A field of force can exist only between

(a) two molecules

(b) two ions

(c) two atoms

(d) two metal particles

78. A substance whose molecules consist of dissimilar atoms is called

(a) semi-conductor

(b) super-conducto

(c) compound

(d) insulator

79. International ohm is defined in terms of the resistance of

(a) a column of mercury

(b) a cube of carbon

(c) a cube of copper

(d) the unit length of wire

80. Three identical resistors are first connected in parallel and then in series.

The resultant resistance of the first combination to the second will be

(a) 9 times

(b) 1/9 times
(c) 1/3 times
(d) 3 times

91. Which method can be used for absolute measurement of resistances ?

(a) Lorentz method
(b) Releigh method
(c) Ohm's law method
(d) Wheatstone bridge method

92. Three 6 ohm resistors are connected to form a triangle. What is the resistance between any two corners ?

(a) 3/2 Q
(b 6 Q
(c) 4 Q
(d) 8/3 Q

93. Ohm's law is not applicable to

(a) semi-conductors
(b) D.C. circuits
(c) small resistors
(d) high currents

94. Two copper conductors have equal length. The cross-sectional area of one conductor is four times that of the other. If the conductor having smaller crosssectional area has a resistance of 40 ohms the resistance of other conductor will be

(a) 160 ohms
(b) 80 ohms
(c) 20 ohms
(d) 10 ohms

95. A nichrome wire used as a heater coil has the resistance of 2 £2/m. For a heater of 1 kW at 200 V, the length of wire required will be

(a) 80 m
(b) 60 m
(c) 40 m
(d) 20 m

96. Temperature co-efficient of resistance is expressed in terms of

(a) ohms/°C
(b) mhos/ohm°C
(c) ohms/ohm°C

98. When current flows through heater coil it glows but supply wiring does not glow because

(a) current through supply line flows at slower speed

(b) supply wiring is covered with insulation layer

(c) resistance of heater coil is more than the supply wires

(d) supply wires are made of superior material

99. The condition for the validity under Ohm's law is that

(a) resistance must be uniform

(b) current should be proportional to the size of the resistance

(c) resistance must be wire wound type

(d) temperature at positive end should be more than the temperature at negative end

100. Which of the following statement is correct ?

(a) A semi-conductor is a material whose conductivity is same as between that of a conductor and an insulator

(b) A semi-conductor is a material which has conductivity having average value of conductivity of metal and insulator

(c) A semi-conductor is one which con¬ducts only half of the applied voltage

(d) A semi-conductor is a material made of alternate layers of conducting material and insulator

101. A rheostat differs from potentiometer in the respect that it

(a) has lower wattage rating

(b) has higher wattage rating

(c) has large number of turns

(d) offers large number of tapping

102. The weight of an aluminium conductor as compared to a copper conductor of identical cross-section, for the same electrical resistance, is

(a) 50%

(b) 60%

(c) 100%

(d) 150%

103. An open resistor, when checked with an ohm-meter reads

(a) zero

(b) infinite

(c) high but within tolerance

(d) low but not zero

104. are the materials having electrical conductivity much less than most of the metals but much greater than that of typical insulators.

(a) Varistors

(b) Thermistor

(c) Semi-conductors

(d) Variable resistors

105. All good conductors have high

(a) conductance

(b) resistance

(c) reluctance

(d) thermal conductivity

106. Voltage dependent resistors are usually made from

(a) charcoal

(b) silicon carbide

(c) nichrome

(d) graphite

107. Voltage dependent resistors are used

(a) for inductive circuits

(b) to supress surges

(c) as heating elements

(d) as current stabilizers

108. The ratio of mass of proton to that of electron is nearly

(a) 1840

(b) 1840

(c) 30

(d) 4

109. The number of electrons in the outer most orbit of carbon atom is

(a) 3

(b) 4

(c) 6

(d) 7

110. With three resistances connected in parallel, if each dissipates 20 W the total power supplied by the voltage source equals

(a) 10 W

(b) 20 W

(c) 40 W

(d) 60 W

111. A thermistor has

(a) positive temperature coefficient

(b) negative temperature coefficient

(c) zero temperature coefficient

(d) variable temperature coefficient

112. If/, R and t are the current, resistance and time respectively, then according

to Joule's law heat produced will be proportional to

(a) I2Rt

(b) I2Rf

(c) I2R2t

(d) I2R2t*

113. Nichrome wire is an alloy of

(a) lead and zinc

(b) chromium and vanadium

(c) nickel and chromium

(d) copper and silver

114. When a voltage of one volt is applied, a circuit allows one micro ampere current to flow through it. The conductance of the circuit is

(a) 1 n-mho

(b) 106 mho

(c) 1 milli-mho

(d) none of the above

115. Which of the following can have negative temperature coefficient ?

(a) Compounds of silver

(6) Liquid metals

(c) Metallic alloys

(d) Electrolytes

116. Conductance : mho ::

(a) resistance : ohm

(b) capacitance : henry

(c) inductance : farad

(d) lumen : steradian

117. 1 angstrom is equal to

(a) 10-8 mm

(b) 10"6 cm

(c) 10"10 m

(d) 10~14 m

118. One newton meter is same as

(a) one watt
(b) one joule
(c) five joules
(d) one joule second
1. The insulating material for a cable should have
(a) low cost
(b) high dielectric strength
(c) high mechanical strength
(d) all of the above
2. Which of the following protects a cable against mechanical injury ?
(a) Bedding
(b) Sheath
(c) Armouring
(d) None of the above
3. Which of the following insulation is used in cables ?
(a) Varnished cambric
(b) Rubber
(c) Paper
(d) Any of the above
4. Empire tape is
(a) varnished cambric
(b) vulcanised rubber
(c) impregnated paper
(d) none of the above
5. The thickness of the layer of insulation on the conductor, in cables, depends upon
(a) reactive power
(b) power factor
(c) voltage
(d) current carrying capacity
6. The bedding on a cable consists of
(a) hessian cloth
(b) jute
(c) any of the above
(d) none of the above
7. The insulating material for cables should
(a) be acid proof
(b) be non-inflammable

(c) be non-hygroscopic
(d) have all above properties
8. In a cable immediately above metallic sheath ______ is provided.
(a) earthing connection
(b) bedding
(c) armouring
(d) none of the above
9. The current carrying capacity of cables in D.C. is more thanthat in A.C. mainly due to
(a) absence of harmonics
(b) non-existence of any stability limit
(c) smaller dielectric loss
(d) absence of ripples
(e) none of the above
10. In case of three core flexible cable the colour of the neutral is
(a) blue
(b) black
(c) brown
(d) none of the above
11 cables are used for 132 kV lines.
(a) High tension
(b) Super tension
(c) Extra high tension
(d) Extra super voltage
12. Conduit pipes are normally used to protect ______ cables.
(a) unsheathed cables
(b) armoured
(c) PVC sheathed cables
(d) all of the above
13. The minimum dielectric stress in a cable is at
(a) armour
(b) bedding
(c) conductor surface
(d) lead sheath
14. In single core cables armouring is not done to
(a) avoid excessive sheath losses
(b) make it flexible
(c) either of the above

(d) none of the above
15. Dielectric strength of rubber is around
(a) 5 kV/mm
(b) 15 kV/mm
(c) 30 kV/mm
(d) 200 kV/mm
16. Low tension cables are generally used up to
(a) 200 V
(b) 500 V
(c) 700 V
(d) 1000 V
17. In a cable, the maximum stress under operating conditions is at
(a) insulation layer
(b) sheath
(c) armour
(d) conductor surface
18. High tension cables are generally used up to
(a) 11kV
(b) 33kV
(c) 66 kV
(d) 132 kV
19. The surge resistance of cable is
(a) 5 ohms
(b) 20 ohms
(c) 50 ohms
(d) 100 ohms
20. PVC stands for
(a) polyvinyl chloride
(b) post varnish conductor
(c) pressed and varnished cloth
(d) positive voltage conductor
21. In the cables, the location of fault is usually found out by comparing
(a) the resistance of the conductor
(b) the inductance of conductors
(c) the capacitances of insulated conductors
(d) all above parameters
22. In capacitance grading of cables we use a ______ dielectric.
(a) composite

(b) porous
(c) homogeneous
(d) hygroscopic
23. Pressure cables are generally not used beyond
(a) 11 kV
(b) 33 kV
(c) 66 kV
(d) 132 kV
24. The material for armouring on cable is usually
(a) steel tape
(b) galvanised steel wire
(c) any of the above
(d) none of the above
25. Cables, generally used beyond 66 kV are
(a) oil filled
(b) S.L. type
(c) belted
(d) armoured
26. The relative permittivity of rubber is
(a) between 2 and 3
(b) between 5 and 6
(c) between 8 and 10
(d) between 12 and 14
27. Solid type cables are considered unreliable beyond 66 kV because
(a) insulation may melt due to higher temperature
(b) skin effect dominates on the conductor
(c) of corona loss between conductor and sheath material
(d) there is a danger of breakdown of insulation due to the presence of voids
28. If the length of a cable is doubled, its capacitance
(a) becomes one-fourth
(b) becomes one-half
(c) becomes double
(d) remains unchanged
29. In cables the charging current
(a) lags the voltage by 90°
(b) leads the voltage by 90°
(c) lags the voltage by 180°

(d) leads the voltage by 180°

30. A certain cable has an insulation of relative permittivity 4. If the insulation is

replaced by one of relative permittivity 2, the capacitance of the cable will become

(a) one half

(6) double

(c) four times

(d) none of the above

31. If a cable of homogeneous insulation has a maximum stress of 10 kV/ mm,

then the dielectric strength of insulation should be

(a) 5 kV/mm

(b) 10 kV/mm

(c) 15 kV/mm

(d) 30 kV/mm

32. In the cables, sheaths are used to

(a) prevent the moisture from entering the cable

(b) provide enough strength

(e) provide proper insulation

(d) none of the above

33. The intersheaths in the cables are used to

(a) minimize the stress

(b) avoid the requirement of good insulation

(c) provide proper stress distribution

(d) none of the above

34. The electrostatic stress in underground cables is

(a) same at the conductor and the sheath

(b) minimum at the conductor and maximum at the sheath

(c) maximum at the conductor and minimum at the sheath

(d) zero at the conductor as well as on the sheath

(e) none of the above

35. The breakdown of insulation of the cable can be avoided economically by the

use of

(a) inter-sheaths

(b) insulating materials with different dielectric constants

(c) both (a) and (b)

(d) none of the above

36. The insulation of the cable decreases with

(a) the increase in length of the insulation

(b) the decrease in the length of the insulation

(c) either (a) or (b)

(d) none of the above

37. A cable carrying alternating current has

(a) hysteresis losses only

(b) hysteresis and leakage losses only

(c) hysteresis, leakage and copper losses only

(d) hysteresis, leakage, copper and friction losses

38. In a cable the voltage stress is maximum at

(a) sheath

(6) insulator

(e) surface of the conductor

(d) core of the conductor

39. Capacitance grading of cable implies

(a) use of dielectrics of different permeabilities

(b) grading according to capacitance of cables per km length

(c) cables using single dielectric in different concentrations

(d) capacitance required to be introduced at different lengths to counter the effect

of inductance

40. Underground cables are laid at sufficient depth

(a) to minimise temperature stresses

(b) to avoid being unearthed easily due to removal of soil

(c) to minimise the effect of shocks and vibrations due to gassing vehicles, etc.

(d) for all of the above reasons

41. The advantage of cables over overhead transmission lines is

(a) easy maintenance

(b) low cost

(c) can be used in congested areas

(d) can be used in high voltage circuits

42. The thickness of metallic shielding on cables is usually

(a) 0.04 mm

(b) 0.2 to 0.4 mm

(e) 3 to 5 mm

(d) 40 to 60 mm

43. Cables for 220 kV lines are invariably

(a) mica insulated

(b) paper insulated

(c) compressed oil or compressed gas insulated

(d) rubber insulated

(e) none of the above

44. Is a cable is to be designed for use on 1000 kV, which insulation would you prefer ?

(a) Polyvinyle chloride

(b) Vulcanised rubber

(c) Impregnated paper

(d) Compressed SFe gas

45. If a power cable and a communication cable are to run parallel the minimum

distance between the two, to avoid interference, should be

(a) 2 cm

(b) 10 cm

(c) 50 cm

(d) 400 cm

46. Copper as conductor for cables is used as

(a) annealed

(b) hardened and tempered

(c) hard drawn

(d) alloy with chromium

47. The insulating material should have

(a) low permittivity

(b) high resistivity

(c) high dielectric strength

(d) all of the above

48. The advantage of oil filled cables is

(a) more perfect impregnation

(b) smaller overall size

(c) no ionisation, oxidation and formation of voids

(d) all of the above

49. The disadvantage with paper as insulating material is

(a) it is hygroscopic

(6) it has high capacitance

(c) it is an organic material
(d) none of the above
50. The breakdown voltage of a cable depends on
(a) presence of moisture
(b) working temperature
(c) time of application of the voltage
(d) <u>all of the above</u>
1. Tesla is a unit of
(a) field strength
(b) inductance
(c) <u>flux density</u>
(d) flux
2. A permeable substance is one
(a) which is a good conductor
(6) which is a bad conductor
(c) which is a strong magnet
(d) <u>through which the magnetic lines of force can pass very easily</u>
3. The materials having low retentivity are suitable for making
(a) weak magnets
(b) <u>temporary magnets</u>
(c) permanent magnets
(d) none of the above
4. A magnetic field exists around
(a) iron
(b) copper
(c) aluminium
(d) <u>moving charges</u>
5. Ferrites are materials.
(a) paramagnetic
(b) diamagnetic
(c) <u>ferromagnetic</u>
(d) none of the above
6. Air gap has________eluctance as compared to iron or steel path
(a) little
(b) <u>lower</u>
(c) higher
(d) zero
7. The direction of magnetic lines of force is

(a) from south pole to north pole
(b) from north pole to south pole
(c) from one end of the magnet to another
(d) none of the above

8. Which of the following is a vector quantity ?
(a) Relative permeability
(b) Magnetic field intensity
(c) Flux density
(d) Magnetic potential

9. The two conductors of a transmission line carry equal current I in opposite
directions. The force on each conductor is
(a) proportional to 7
(b) proportional to X
(c) proportional to distance between the conductors
(d) inversely proportional to I

10. A material which is slightly repelled by a magnetic field is known as
(a) ferromagnetic material
(b) diamagnetic material
(c) paramagnetic material
(d) conducting material

11. When an iron piece is placed in a magnetic field
(a) the magnetic lines of force will bend away from their usual paths in order to go
away from the piece
(b) the magnetic lines of force will bend away from their usual paths in order to
pass through the piece
(c) the magnetic field will not be affected
(d) the iron piece will break

12. Fleming's left hand rule is used to find
(a) direction of magnetic field due to current carrying conductor
(b) direction of flux in a solenoid
(c) direction of force on a current carrying conductor in a magnetic field
(d) polarity of a magnetic pole

13. The ratio of intensity of magnetisation to the magnetisation force is known as
(a) flux density

(b) susceptibility
(c) relative permeability
(d) none of the above
14. Magnetising steel is normals difficult because
(a) it corrodes easily
(6) it has high permeability
(c) it has high specific gravity
(d) it has low permeability
15. The left hand rule correlates to
(a) current, induced e.m.f. and direction of force on a conductor
(b) magnetic field, electric field and direction of force on a conductor
(c) self induction, mutual induction and direction of force on a conductor
(d) current, magnetic field and direction of force on a conductor
16. The unit of relative permeability is
(a) henry/metre
(b) henry
(c) henry/sq. m
(d) it is dimensionless
17. A conductor of length L has current I passing through it, when it is placed
parallel to a magnetic field. The force experienced by the conductor will be
(a) zero
(b) BLI
(c) B2LI
(d) BLI2
18. The force between two long parallel conductors is inversely proportional to
(a) radius of conductors
(b) current in one conductor
(c) product of current in two conductors
(d) distance between the conductors
19. Materials subjected to rapid reversal of magnetism should have
(a) large area oiB-H loop
(b) high permeability and low hysteresis loss
(c) high co-ercivity and high retentivity
(d) high co-ercivity and low density

20. Indicate which of the following material does not retain magnetism permanently.
(a) Soft iron
(b) Stainless steel
(e) Hardened steel
(d) None of the above
21. The main constituent of permalloy is
(a) cobalt
(b) chromium
(c) nickel
(d) tungsten
22. The use of permanent magnets is. not made in
(a) magnetoes
(6) energy meters
(c) transformers
(d) loud-speakers
23. Paramagnetic materials have relative permeability
(a) slightly less than unity
(b) equal to unity
(c) slightly more than unity
(d) equal to that ferromagnetic mate rials
25. Substances which have permeability less than the permeability of free space
are known as
(a) ferromagnetic
(b) paramagnetic
(c) diamagnetic
(d) bipolar
27. In the left hand rule, forefinger always represents
(a) voltage
(b) current
(c) magnetic field
(d) direction of force on the conductor
28. Which of the following is a ferromagnetic material ?
(a) Tungsten
(b) Aluminium
(c) Copper
(d) Nickel

29. Ferrites are a sub-group of
(a) non-magnetic materials
(6) ferro-magnetic materials
(c) paramagnetic materials
(d) <u>ferri-magnetic materials</u>
30. Gilbert is a unit of
(a) electromotive force
(b) <u>magnetomotive force</u>
(c) conductance
(d) permittivity
51. Unit for quantity of electricity is
(a) ampere-hour
(b) watt
(c) joule
(d) <u>coulomb</u>
52. The Biot-savart's law is a general modification of
(a) Kirchhoffs law
(b) Lenz's law
(c) <u>Ampere's law</u>
(d) Faraday's laws
53. The most effective and quickest may of making a magnet from soft iron is by
(a) <u>placing it inside a coil carrying current</u>
(b) induction
(c) the use of permanent magnet
(d) rubbing with another magnet
54. The commonly used material for shielding or screening magnetism is
(a) copper
(b) aluminium
(c) <u>soft iron</u>
(d) brass
55. If a copper disc is rotated rapidly below a freely suspended magnetic needle,
the magnetic needle shall start rotating with a velocity
(a) less than that of disc but in opposite direction
(b) equal to that of disc and in the same direction
(c) equal to that of disc and in the opposite direction
(d) <u>less than that of disc and in the same direction</u>

56. A permanent magnet
(a) attracts some substances and repels others
(b) attracts all paramagnetic substances and repels others
(c) attracts only ferromagnetic substances
(d) attracts ferromagnetic substances and repels all others
57. The retentivity (a property) of material is useful for the construction of
(a) permanent magnets
(b) transformers
(c) non-magnetic substances
(d) electromagnets
58. The relative permeability of materials is not constant.
(a) diamagnetic
(b) paramagnetic
(c) ferromagnetic
(d) insulating
59. The materials are a bit inferior conductors of magnetic flux than air.
(a) ferromagnetic
(b) paramagnetic
(c) diamagnetic
(d) dielectric
60. Hysteresis loop in case of magnetically hard materials is more in shape as
compared to magnetically soft materials.
(a) circular
(b) triangular
(c) rectangular
(d) none of the above
61. A rectangular magnet of magnetic moment M is cut into two piece of same
length, the magnetic moment of each piece will be
(a) M
(b) M/2
(c) 2 M
(d) M/4
62. A keeper is used to
(a) change the direction of magnetic lines
(b) amplify flux

(c) restore lost flux

(d) provide a closed path for flux

63. Magnetic moment is a

(a) pole strength

(6) universal constant

(c) scalar quantity

(d) vector quantity

64. The change of cross-sectional area of conductor in magnetic field will affect

(a) reluctance of conductor

(b) resistance of conductor

(c) (a) and (b) both in the same way

(d) none of the above

65. The uniform magnetic field is

(a) the field of a set of parallel conductors

(b) the field of a single conductor

(c) the field in which all lines of magnetic flux are parallel and equidistant

(d) none of the above

66. The magneto-motive force is

(a) the voltage across the two ends of exciting coil

(b) the flow of an electric current

(c) the sum of all currents embraced by one line of magnetic field

(d) the passage of magnetic field through an exciting coil

91. For which of the following materials the saturation value is the highest ?

(a) Ferromagnetic materials

(6) Paramagnetic materials

(c) Diamagnetic materials

(d) Ferrites

92. The magnetic materials exhibit the property of magnetisation because of

(a) orbital motion of electrons

(b) spin of electrons

(c) spin of nucleus

(d) either of these

93. For which of the following materials the net magnetic moment should be zero ?

(a) Diamagnetic materials

(b) Ferrimagnetic materials

(c) Antiferromagnetic materials

(d) Antiferrimagnetic materials

94. The attraction capacity of electromagnet will increase if the

(a) core length increases i

(b) core area increases

(c) flux density decreases

(d) flux density increases

95. Which of the following statements is correct ?

(a) The conductivity of ferrites is better than ferromagnetic materials

(b) The conductivity of ferromagnetic materials is better than ferrites

(c) The conductivity of ferrites is very high

(d) The conductivity of ferrites is same as that of ferromagnetic materials

96. Temporary magnets are used in

(a) loud-speakers

(b) generators

(c) motors

(d) all of the above

97. Main causes of noisy solenoid are

(a) strong tendency of fan out of laminations at the end caused by repulsion among magnetic lines of force

(b) uneven bearing surface, caused by dirt or uneven wear between moving and stationary parts

(c) both of above

(d) none of the above

99. Core of an electromagnet should have

(a) low coercivity

(6) high susceptibility

(c) both of the above

(d) none of the above

100. Magnetism of a magnet can be destroyed by

(a) heating

(b) hammering

(c) by inductive action of another magnet

(d) by all above methods

1. "The mass of an ion liberated at an electrode is directly proportional to the quantity of electricity".

The above statement is associated with

(a) Newton's law

(b) Faraday's law of electromagnetic

(c) Faraday's law of electrolysis

(d) Gauss's law

2. The charge required to liberate one gram equivalent of any substance is known as ______ constant

(a) time

(b) Faraday's

(c) Boltzman

3. During the charging of a lead-acid cell

(a) its voltage increases

(b) it gives out energy

(c) its cathode becomes dark chocolate brown in colour

(d) specific gravity of H2SO4 decreases

4. The capacity of a lead-acid cell does not depend on its

(a) temperature

(b) rate of charge

(c) rate of discharge

(d) quantity of active material

5. During charging the specific gravity of the electrolyte of a lead-acid battery

(a) increases

(b) decreases

(c) remains the same

(d) becomes zero

6. The active materials on the positive and negative plates of a fully charged leadacid battery are

(a) lead and lead peroxide

(b) lead sulphate and lead

(c) lead peroxide and lead

(d) none of the above

7. When a lead-acid battery is in fully charged condition, the colour of its positive

plate is

(a) dark grey
(b) brown
(c) dark brown
(d) none of above

8. The active materials of a nickel-iron battery are
(a) nickel hydroxide
(6) powdered iron and its oxide
(c) 21% solution of KOH
(d) all of the above

9. The ratio of ampere-hour efficiency to watt-hour efficiency of a lead-acid cell is
(a) just one
(b) always greater than one
(c) always less than one
(d) none of the above.

10. The best indication about the state of charge on a lead-acid battery is given by
(a) output voltage
(b) temperature of electrolyte
(c) specific gravity of electrolyte
(d) none of the above

11. The storage battery generally used in electric power station is
(a) nickel-cadmium battery
(b) zinc-carbon battery
(c) lead-acid battery
(d) none of the above

12. The output voltage of a charger is
(a) less than the battery voltage
(b) higher than the battery voltage
(c) the same as the battery voltage
(d) none of the above

13. Cells are connected in series in order to
(a) increase the voltage rating
(6) increase the current rating
(c) increase the life of the cells
(d) none of the above

14. Five 2 V cells are connected in parallel. The output voltage is
(a) 1 V

(6) 1.5 V

(c) 1.75 V

(d) 2 V

15. The capacity of a battery is expressed in terms of

(a) current rating

(b) voltage rating

(c) ampere-hour rating

(d) none of the above

16. Duringthe charging and discharging of a nickel-iron cell

(a) corrosive fumes are produced

(b) water is neither formed nor absorbed

(c) nickel hydroxide remains unsplit

(d) its e.m.f. remains constant

17. As compared to constant-current system, the constant-voltage system of charging a lead acid cell has the advantage of

(a) reducing time of charging

(b) increasing cell capacity

(c) both (a) and (b)

(d) avoiding excessive gassing

18. A dead storage battery can be revived by

(a) adding distilled water

(6) adding so-called battery restorer

(c) a dose of H2SO4

(d) none of the above

19. As compared to a lead-acid cell, the efficiency of a nickel-iron cell is less due to its

(a) compactness

(b) lower e.m.f.

(c) small quantity of electrolyte used

(d) higher internal resistance

20. Trickle charging of a storage battery helps to

(a) maintain proper electrolyte level

(b) increase its reserve capacity

(c) prevent sulphation

(d) keep it fresh and fully charged

21. Those substances of the cell which take active part in chemical combination and hence produce electricity during charging or discharging are known as_______materials.

(a) passive
(b) active
(c) redundant
(d) inert

22. In a lead-acid cell dilute sulphuric acid (electrolyte) approximately comprises the following
(a) one part H2O, three parts H2SO4
(b) two parts H2O, two parts H2SO4
(c) three parts H2O, one part H2SO4
(d) all H2S04

23. It is noticed that durum charging
(a) there is a rise in voltage
(b) energy is absorbed by the cell
(c) specific gravity of H2SO4 is increased
(d) all of the above

24. It is noticed that during discharging the following does not happen
(a) both anode and cathode become PbS04
(b) specific gravity of H2SO4 decreases
(c) voltage of the cell decreases
(d) the cell absorbs energy

25. The ampere-hour efficiency of a leadacid cell is normally between
(a) 20 to 30%
(b) 40 to 50%
(c) 60 to 70%
(d) 90 to 95%

26. The watt-hour efficiency of a lead-acid cell varies between
(a) 25 to 35%
(b) 40 to 60%
(c) 70 to 80%
(d) 90 to 95%

27. The capacity of a lead-acid cell is measured in
(a) amperes
(b) ampere-hours
(c) watts
(d) watt-hours

28. The capacity of a lead-acid cell depends on
(a) rate of discharge
(b) temperature

(c) density of electrolyte

(d) all above

29. When the lead-acid cell is fully charged, the electrolyte assumes ______appearance

(a) dull

(b) reddish

(c) bright

(d) milky

30. The e.m.f. of an Edison cell, when fully charged, is nearly

(a) 1.4 V

(b) 1 V

(c) 0.9 V

(d) 0.8 V

31. The internal resistance of an alkali cell is nearly ______ times that of the leadacid cell.

(a) two

(b) three

(c) four

(d) five

32. The average charging voltage for alkali cell is about

(a) 1 V

(b) 1.2 V

(c) 1.7 V

(d) 2.1 V

33. On the average the ampere-hour efficiency of an Edison cell is about

(a) 40%

(b) 60%

(c) 70%

(d) 80%

34. The active material of the positive plates of silver-zinc batteries is

(a) silver oxide

(b) lead oxide

(c) lead

(d) zinc powder

35. Lead-acid cell has a life of nearly charges and discharges

(a) 500

(b) 700

(c) 1000

(d) 1250

36. Life of the Edison cell is at least

(a) five years

(b) seven years

(c) eight years

(d) ten years

37. The internal resistance of a lead-acid cell is that of Edison cell

(a) less than

(b) more than

(c) equal to

(d) none of the above

38. Electrolyte used in an Edison cell is

(a) NaOH

(b) KOH

(c) HC1

(d) HN03

39. Electrolyte used in a lead-acid cell is

(a) NaOH

(b) onlyH2S04

(c) only water

(d) dilute H2SO4

40. Negative plate of an Edison cell is made of

(a) copper

(b) lead

(c) iron

(d) silver oxide

41. The open circuit voltage of any storage cell depends wholly upon

(a) its chemical constituents

(b) on the strength of its electrolyte

(c) its temperature

(d) all above

42. The specific gravity of electrolyte is measured by

(a) manometer

(6) a mechanical gauge

(c) hydrometer

(d) psychrometer

43. When the specific gravity of the electrolyte of a lead-acid cell is reduced to 1.1 to 1.15 the cell is in

(a) charged state
(b) discharged state
(c) both (a) and (b)
(d) active state

44. In _______ system the charging current is intermittently controlled at either a
maximum or minimum value
(a) two rate charge control
(b) trickle charge
(c) floating charge
(d) an equalizing charge

45. Over charging
(a) produces excessive gassing
(b) loosens the active material
(e) increases the temperature resulting in buckling of plates
(d) all above

46. Undercharging
(a) reduces specific gravity of the electrolyte
(b) increases specific gravity of the electrolyte
(c) produces excessive gassing
(d) increases the temperature

47. Internal short circuits are caused by
(a) breakdown of one or more separators
(b) excess accumulation of sediment at the bottom of the cell
(c) both (a) and (b)
(d) none of the above

48. The effect of sulphation is that the internal resistance
(a) increases
(b) decreases
(c) remains same
(d) none of the above

49. Excessive formation of lead sulphate on the surface of the plates happens because of
(a) allowing a battery to stand in discharged condition for a long time
(b) topping up with electrolyte
(c) persistent undercharging
(d) all above

50. The substances which combine together to store electrical energy during the charge are called _______ materials

(a) active

(b) passive

(c) inert

(d) dielectric

1. Which of the following does not change in a transformer ?

(a) Current

(b) Voltage

(c) Frequency

(d) All of the above

2. In a transformer the energy is conveyed from primary to secondary

(a) through cooling coil

(b) through air

(c) by the flux

(d) none of the above

3. A transformer core is laminated to

(a) reduce hysteresis loss

(b) reduce eddy current losses

(c) reduce copper losses

(d) reduce all above losses

4. The degree of mechanical vibrations produced by the laminations of a transformer depends on

(a) tightness of clamping

(b) gauge of laminations

(c) size of laminations

(d) all of the above

5. The no-load current drawn by transformer is usually what per cent of the full load current ?

(a) 0.2 to 0.5 per cent

(b) 2 to 5 per cent

(c) 12 to 15 per cent

(d) 20 to 30 per cent

6. The path of a magnetic flux in a transformer should have

(a) high resistance

(b) high reluctance

(c) low resistance

(d) low reluctance

7. No-load on a transformer is carried out to determine
(a) copper loss
(b) magnetising current
(c) magnetising current and loss
(d) efficiency of the transformer
8. The dielectric strength of transformer oil is expected to be
(a) lkV
(b) 33 kV
(c) 100 kV
(d) 330 kV
9. Sumpner's test is conducted on trans-formers to determine
(a) temperature
(b) stray losses
(c) all-day efficiency
(d) none of the above
10. The permissible flux density in case of cold rolled grain oriented steel is around
(a) 1.7 Wb/m2
(b) 2.7 Wb/m2
(c) 3.7 Wb/m2
(d) 4.7 Wb/m2
11. The efficiency of a transformer will be maximum when
(a) copper losses = hysteresis losses
(b) hysteresis losses = eddy current losses
(c) eddy current losses = copper losses
(d) copper losses = iron losses
12. No-load current in a transformer
(a) lags behind the voltage by about 75°
(b) leads the voltage by about 75°
(c) lags behind the voltage by about 15°
(d) leads the voltage by about 15°
13. The purpose of providing an iron core in a transformer is to
(a) provide support to windings
(b) reduce hysteresis loss
(c) decrease the reluctance of the magnetic path
(d) reduce eddy current losses
14. Which of the following is not a part of transformer installation ?
(a) Conservator

(b) Breather

(c) Buchholz relay

(d) Exciter

15. While conducting short-circuit test on a transformer the following side is short circuited

(a) High voltage side

(b) Low voltage side

(c) Primary side

(d) Secondary side

16. In the transformer following winding has got more cross-sectional area

(a) Low voltage winding

(b) High voltage winding

(c) Primary winding

(d) Secondary winding

17. A transformer transforms

(a) voltage

(b) current

(c) power

(d) frequency

18. A transformer cannot raise or lower the voltage of a D.C. supply because

(a) there is no need to change the D.C. voltage

(b) a D.C. circuit has more losses

(c) Faraday's laws of electromagnetic induction are not valid since the rate of change of flux is zero

(d) none of the above

19. Primary winding of a transformer

(a) is always a low voltage winding

(b) is always a high voltage winding

(c) could either be a low voltage or high voltage winding

(d) none of the above

20. Which winding in a transformer has more number of turns ?

(a) Low voltage winding

(b) High voltage winding

(c) Primary winding

(d) Secondary winding

21. Efficiency of a power transformer is of the order of

(a) 100 per cent
(b) 98 per cent
(c) 50 per cent
(d) 25 per cent

22. In a given transformer for given applied voltage, losses which remain constant irrespective of load changes are
(a) friction and windage losses
(b) copper losses
(c) hysteresis and eddy current losses
(d) none of the above

23. A common method of cooling a power transformer is
(a) natural air cooling
(b) air blast cooling
(c) oil cooling
(d) any of the above

24. The no load current in a transformer lags behind the applied voltage by an angle of about
(a) 180°
(b) 120″
(c) 90°
(d) 75°

25. In a transformer routine efficiency depends upon
(a) supply frequency
(b) load current
(c) power factor of load
(d) both (b) and (c)

26. In the transformer the function of a conservator is to
(a) provide fresh air for cooling the transformer
(b) supply cooling oil to transformer in time of need
(c) protect the transformer from damage when oil expends due to heating
(d) none of the above

27. Natural oil cooling is used for transformers up to a rating of
(a) 3000 kVA
(b) 1000 kVA
(c) 500 kVA
(d) 250 kVA

28. Power transformers are designed to have maximum efficiency at

(a) nearly full load
(b) 70% full load
(c) 50% full load
(d) no load
29. The maximum efficiency of a distribution transformer is
(a) at no load
(b) at 50% full load
(c) at 80% full load
(d) at full load
30. Transformer breaths in when
(a) load on it increases
(b) load on it decreases
(c) load remains constant
(d) none of the above
31. No-load current of a transformer has
(a) has high magnitude and low power factor
(b) has high magnitude and high power factor
(c) has small magnitude and high power factor
(d) has small magnitude and low power factor
32. Spacers are provided between adjacent coils
(a) to provide free passage to the cooling oil
(b) to insulate the coils from each other
(c) both (a) and (b)
(d) none of the above
33. Greater the secondary leakage flux
(a) less will be the secondary induced e.m.f.
(b) less will be the primary induced e.m.f.
(c) less will be the primary terminal voltage
(d) none of the above
34. The purpose of providing iron core in a step-up transformer is
(a) to provide coupling between primary and secondary
(b) to increase the magnitude of mutual flux
(c) to decrease the magnitude of mag-netizing current
(d) to provide all above features
35. The power transformer is a constant
(a) voltage device
(b) current device
(c) power device

(d) main flux device

36. Two transformers operating in parallel will share the load depending upon their

(a) leakage reactance

(b) per unit impedance

(c) efficiencies

(d) ratings

37. If R2 is the resistance of secondary winding of the transformer and K is the transformation ratio then the equivalent secondary resistance referred to primary will be

(a) R2/VK

(b) R2IK2

(c) R22!K2

(d) R22/K

38. What will happen if the transformers working in parallel are not connected with regard to polarity ?

(a) The power factor of the two trans-formers will be different from the power factor of common load

(b) Incorrect polarity will result in dead short circuit

(c) The transformers will not share load in proportion to their kVA ratings

(d) none of the above

39. If the percentage impedances of the two transformers working in parallel are different, then

(a) transformers will be overheated

(b) power factors of both the transformers will be same

(c) parallel operation will be not possible

(d) parallel operation will still be possible, but the power factors at which the two transformers operate will be different from the power factor of the common load

40. In a transformer the tappings are generally provided on

(a) primary side

(b) secondary side

(c) low voltage side

(d) high voltage side

41. The use of higher flux density in the transformer design

(a) reduces weight per kVA

(6) reduces iron losses

(c) reduces copper losses

(d) increases part load efficiency

42. The chemical used in breather for transformer should have the quality of

(a) ionizing air

(b) absorbing moisture

(c) cleansing the transformer oil

(d) cooling the transformer oil.

43. The chemical used in breather is

(a) asbestos fiber

(b) silica sand

(c) sodium chloride

(d) silica gel

45. The transformer ratings are usually expressed in terms of

(a) volts

(b) amperes

(c) kW

(d) kVA

46. The noise resulting from vibrations of laminations set by magnetic forces, is termed as

(a) magnetostrication

(b) boo

(c) hum

(d) zoom

47. Hysteresis loss in a transformer varies as CBmax = maximum flux density)

(a) Bmax

(b) Bmax1-6

(C) Bmax1-83

(d) B max

48. Material used for construction of transformer core is usually

(a) wood

(b) copper

(c) aluminium

(d) silicon steel

49. The thickness of laminations used in a transformer is usually

(a) 0.4 mm to 0.5 mm

(b) 4 mm to 5 mm

(c) 14 mm to 15 mm

(d) 25 mm to 40 mm

50. The function of conservator in a transformer is

(a) to project against'internal fault

(b) to reduce copper as well as core losses

(c) to cool the transformer oil

(d) to take care of the expansion and contraction of transformer oil due to variation of temperature of sur-roundings

51. The highest voltage for transmitting electrical power in India is

(a) 33 kV.

(6) 66 kV

(c) 132 kV

(d) 400 kV

52. In a transformer the resistance between its primary and secondary is

(a) zero

(b) 1 ohm

(c) 1000 ohms

(d) infinite

53. A transformer oil must be free from

(a) sludge

(b) odour

(c) gases

(d) moisture

54. A Buchholz relay can be installed on

(a) auto-transformers

(b) air-cooled transformers

(c) welding transformers

(d) oil cooled transformers

55. Gas is usually not liberated due to dissociation of transformer oil unless the oil temperature exceeds

(a) 50°C

(b) 80°C

(c) 100°C

(d) 150°C

56. The main reason for generation of harmonics in a transformer could be

(a) fluctuating load

(b) poor insulation

(c) mechanical vibrations

(d) saturation of core

57. Distribution transformers are generally designed for maximum efficiency around

(a) 90% load

(b) zero load

(c) 25% load

(d) 50% load

58. Which of the following property is not necessarily desirable in the material for transformer core ?

(a) Mechanical strength

(6) Low hysteresis loss

(c) High thermal conductivity

(d) High permeability

59. Star/star transformers work satisfactorily when

(a) load is unbalanced only

(b) load is balanced only

(c) on balanced as well as unbalanced loads

(d) none of the above

60. Delta/star transformer works satisfactorily when

(a) load is balanced only

(b) load is unbalanced only

(c) on balanced as well as unbalanced loads

(d) none of the above

61. Buchholz's relay gives warning and protection against

(a) electrical fault inside the transformer itself

(b) electrical fault outside the transformer in outgoing feeder

(c) for both outside and inside faults

(d) none of the above

62. The magnetising current of a transformer is usually small because it has

(a) small air gap

(b) large leakage flux

(c) laminated silicon steel core

(d) fewer rotating parts

63. Which of the following does not change in an ordinary transformer ?

(a) Frequency

(b) Voltage

(c) Current

(d) Any of the above

64. Which of the following properties is not necessarily desirable for the material for transformer core ?

(a) Low hysteresis loss

(b) High permeability

(c) High thermal conductivity

(d) Adequate mechanical strength

65. The leakage flux in a transformer depends upon

(a) load current

(b) load current and voltage

(c) load current, voltage and frequency

(d) load current, voltage, frequency and power factor

66. The path of the magnetic flux in transformer should have

(a) high reluctance

(b) low reactance

(c) high resistance

(d) low resistance

67. Noise level test in a transformer is a

(a) special test

(b) routine test

(c) type test

(d) none of the above

68. Which of the following is not a routine test on transformers ?

(a) Core insulation voltage test

(b) Impedance test

(c) Radio interference test

(d) Polarity test

69. A transformer can have zero voltage regulation at

(a) leading power factor

(b) lagging power factor

(c) unity power factor

(d) zero power factor

70. Helical coils can be used on

(a) low voltage side of high kVA transformers

(b) high frequency transformers

(c) high voltage side of small capacity transformers

(d) high voltage side of high kVA rating transformers

85] A heater draws a current of 8A when connected to a 240V source] What is the resistance value of the heater element in ohms?

A] 40

B] 20

C] 30

D] 60

86] An electric soldering iron with an 80 ohms heating element is plugged into a 240V outlet] How much current will be drawn by the iron?

A] 2A

B] 3A

C] 4A

D] 5A

87] The alternator in a car delivers 4A and has a load of 3 ohms connected across its terminals] Find the voltage of the circuit

A] 18V

B] 24V

C] 12V

D] 16V

88] Three resistors of 1K ohms, 2K ohms and 7K ohms are connected in series with a 30 V supply] If 2 K ohms and 7 K ohms resistors are open circuited, a voltmeter connected across the 7K ohms resistor will indicate...

A] 10 k ohms, 3A

B] 10 k ohms, 300mA

C] 10 k ohms, 3 mA

D] 5 k ohms, 6 mA

89] A voltage source produces an IR drop of 40V across a 20 ohms resistance, 60V across a 30 ohms resistance and 180V across a 90 ohms resistance all in series] How much is the applied voltage?

A] 180 V

B] 240 V

C] 100 V

D] 280 V

90] Three resistors 27 ohms, 47 ohms and 68 ohms are connected in parallel] What is the otal resistance?

A] less than 27 ohms

B] greater than 68 ohms

C] between 27 and 47 ohms

D] sum of all the three resistances

91] One million and one mege ohms resistors are there if connected both in parallel, what would be the combined resistance value?

A] 0.5 mega ohm

B] 0.5 milli ohm

C] 0.5 kilo ohm

D] 0.5 ohm

92] A 24 ohms and a 8 ohms resistors in parallel gets a combined resistance of...

A] 6 ohms

B] 12 ohms

C] 3 ohms

D] 32 ohms

93] Resistors of the following values are connected in parallel, 5 ohms, 5 kilo-ohms, 50 kilo-ohms, 5 mega ohms] Their equivalent resistance will be very near to...

A] 4.5 ohms

B] 4500 ohms

C] 45000 ohms

D] 4,500,000 ohms

94] The resistance of given wire is 2 ohms] The resistance of the other wire made of the same material having twice the length and twice the cross sectional area is...

A] 5 ohms

B] 6 ohms

C] 2 ohms

D] 8 ohms

95] If the area of a metal wire of a given length is doubles, its resistance will...

A] be doubled

B] be halved

C] remain the same

D] be four times more

96].Among the following only one is regarded as resistance wire

A] gold

B] silver

C] nichrome

D] copper

97] Arc heating occurs when the air between electrodes of opposite polarity becomes..

A] moistened

B] dry

C] ionized

D] none of the above

98] The meter used to measure the temperature of furnace is...

A] hydrometer

B] pyrometer

C] hygrometer

D] tachometer

99] in the case of electrolyte a rise in temperature causes...

A] decrease in resistance

B] increase in resistance

C] no change in resistance

D] none of the above

100] Heat developed in a conductor is proportional to the...

A] square of the power

B] square of the resistance

C] square of the current

D] square of the time

101] Out of the four metal/alloys given below, one has almost no change in resistance for temperature change...

A] nickel

B] nichrome

C] platinum

D] manganin

102] A material that is slightly repelled by a magnet is called ...

A] magnetic

B] paramagnetic

C] diamagnetic

D] ferromagnetic

103] A material that can be magnetized only very slightly is called...

A] magnetic

B] paramagnetic

C] diamagnetic

D] ferromagnetic

104] Substances that can be magnetized easily and make very strong magnets are called...

A] ferromagnetic

B] diamagnetic

C] paramagnetic

D] permanent magnetic

105] A substance that has a high retentivity can be used for the manufacture of...

A] electromagnets

B] permanent magnets

C] temporary magnets

D] paramagnets

106] A substance that has low retentivity can be used for the manufacture of...

A] electromagnets

B] permanent magnets

C] bar magnets

D] paramagnets

107] The symbol for inductance is...

A] H

B] I

C] L

D] X

108] Tube lamp choke is the best example of...

A] open circuited

B] short circuited

C] grounded

D] connected to the neutral line

109] The initial function of a choke in a tube light circuit is to...

A] limit the starting current

B] induce high voltage

C] heat up the filament

D] limit the current after starting

110] The second function of a choke in a tube light circuit is to...

A] limit the starting current

B] induce high voltage

C] heat up the filament

D] limit the current after starting

111] The periodic time of a wave from is 2ms] Calculate the frequency

A] 50 HZ

B] 5 HZ

C] <u>500HZ</u>

D] 5 KHZ

112] How big is the peak amplitude of a sine-wave with an effective value of 220 volts?

A] <u>311 V</u>

B] 380 V

C] 400 V

D] 440 V

113] The peak-to-peak voltage is 99V] how big is the effective value of the sine wave?

A] 70 V

B] 44.5V

C] 49.5 V

D] <u>35 V</u>

114] A moving coil voltmeter reads 10 V AC] How big is the effective voltage?

A] higher

B] lower

C] <u>the same</u>

D] 10% higher

115] A moving iron ammeter reads 10 A] how big is the peak current of the oscillation?

A] 7.07 A

B] 1.1414A

C] 70.7 A

D] <u>14.1 A</u>

116] A current of 2 amps flows through a resistance of 10 ohms] The power dissipated in the resistance is equal to...

A] 20 watts

B] 200 watts

C] <u>40 watts</u>

D] 5 watts

117] If the frequency changes from 50 HZ to 100 HZ keeping voltage constant, the inductive reactance of coil connected to supply...

A] remains same

B] become half

C] become doubled

D] become 4 times

118] Capacitance is not affected by...

A] plate area

B] distance between plates

C] dialectic material

D] frequency

119] The capacitive reactance of a capacitor varies...

A] directly with frequency

B] inversely with frequency

C] directly with applied voltage

D] inversely with applied voltage

120] A capacitor acquired 3 coulombs of charge when 6 volts are applied across it] It has a capacitance of ...

A] 0.5 farad

B] 3 farads

C] 3 farads

D] 18 farads

121] A capacitor is connected across a 200 volt AC line, its minimum voltage rating should be...

A] 100 volts

B] 200 Volts

C] 300 volts

D] 400 volts

122] when testing a capacitor with an ohmmeter, the meter indicates some resistance] The capacitor under test is...

A] leaky

B] open

C] good

D] short

123] The total capacitance of a 40 micro farad capacitor connected in series with an 80 micro farad capacitor is...

A] 26.7 micro farad

B] 40 micro farad

C] 60.6 micro farad

D] 120 micro farad

124] For obtaining 1 micro farad capacitor from 3 nos] of 3 micro farad capacitors we have to connect...

A] all in parallel

B] <u>all in series</u>

C] 2 series and one in parallel

D] none of the above

125] In an AC series circuit having R and C the current flowing through the capacitor will be...

A] lagging the voltage

B] <u>leading the voltage</u>

C] in phase with the voltage

D] none of the above

126] If the frequency of the supply is increased in the R-C series circuit the capacitive reactance will be

A] <u>reduced</u>

B] increased

C] having no effect

D] none of the above

127] Power companies are interested in improving the power factor to

A] <u>reduce line current</u>

B] increase motor efficiency

C] increase volt-amperes

D] decrease power

128] A capacitor increases the power factor value of an AC motor load when it is connected...

A] in series with the motor

B] in series with the starter

C<u>] in parallel with the motor</u>

D] in series with the main winding

129] Normally, the power factor of an incandescent lighting circuit is..

A] 0

B] 0.5

C] 0.707

D] <u>1.0</u>

130] When resistance alone is used to determine current in an RLC series circuit, the circuit is...

A] an inductive circuit

B] a capacitive circuit

C] a combination circuit

D] a resonant circuit

131] Inductive reactance is directly related to..

A] resistance

B] frequency

C] capacitance

D] power

132] Synchronous motor when used for power factor improvement should be...

A] under excited

B] over excited

C] loaded

D] running at no load

133] In a RL parallel circuit, the opposition to total current is called...

A] reactance

B] resistance

C] a vector sum

D] impedance

134] In a AC parallel RL circuit, the power dissipated at the

A] impedance

B] resistance

C] inductance

D] capacitance

135] How much is the nominal output voltage of a carbon zinc cell?

A] 12V

B] 1.5V

C] 2.0V

D] 2.2V

136] Cells are connected in series to..

A] increase the output voltage

B] decreases the output voltage

C] decrease the internal resistance

D] increase the current capacity

54137connected in

A] series

B] parallel

C] series-parallel

D] parallel-series

138] The capacity of a cell is measured in

A] watt-hour

B] watts

C] amperes

D] ampere-hour

139] The primary cell which has the shortest shelf life is

A] carbon – zinc

B] alkaline

C] mercury

D] lithium

140] The cell which has very high energy density for given weight or volume to

A] carbon-zinc

B] alkaline

C] mercury

D] lithium

141] A 100-Ah capacity battery should deliver a current of 8A for approximately...

A] 12 h

B] 8 h

C] 20 h

D] 100 h

142] When the battery is needed to be kept idle for a long time...

A] overcharge the battery

B] remove electrolyte

C] clean the plates with distilled water

D] dry them and store the battery in cool dry clean place

143] The active materials of the nickel iron cell are...

A] nickel hydroxide

B] powdered iron and its oxide

C] 21% solution of caustic potash

D] all the above materials

144] The capacity of a cell is measured in

A] watt hour

B] watts

C] amperes

D] ampere-hour

145] To charge a secondary cell, the system used is

A] low voltage AC

B] high voltage AC

C] AC

D] DC

146] What is the number of phases in a normal industrial supply system?

A] one

B] three

C] four

D] two

147] In a 3 phase star connected alternator, the coils have a phase difference of...

A] 120°

B] 240°

C] 60°

D] 360°

148] Delta connection is used no one of the following

A] primary of the transmission line transformer

B] alternator winding

C] secondary of the distribution transformer

D] primary of the distribution transformer

149] Which method can be used to measure the power in a 3-phase unbalanced load system?

A] one wattmeter method

B] tow wattmeter method

C] three wattmeter method

D] three ammeter method

150] Two wattmeters can be used to measure 3-hase power in a 3-phase, 3 wire system with...

A] balanced load

B] unbalanced load

C] balanced as well as unbalanced load

D] out of balanced load

151] A single wattmeter can be used to measure power in a 3-phase system only when the load is..

A] balanaced

B] unbalanced

C] balanced as well as unbalanced load

D] constant

152] The force producing movement of the pointer in an indicating instrument is called as...

A] deflecting force

B] controlling force

C] damping force

D] distracting force

153] A permanent magnet moving coil instrument will read...

A] only AC quantities

B] only DC quantities

C] both AC and DC quantities

D] pulsating quantities

154] An instrument using gravity control will read correctly if used in..

A] vertical position only

B] horizontal position only

C] inclined position only

D] any position

155] Which one of the following damping methods is used in permanent magnet moving coil instrument?

A] air damping

B] fluid damping

C] spring damping

D] eddy current damping

156] Moving coil instrument works on the effect of...

A] chemical effect

B] heating effect

C] electrostatic effect

D] electromagnetic effect

157] The meter installed at your house to measure electrical energy is an example of...

A] indication type instrument

B] recording type instrument

C] indicating as well as recording type instrument

D] integrating type instrument

158].Which of the following material is preferred for permanent magnet?

A] alnico

B] y-alloy

C] silicon steel

D] wrought iron

159] The instrument which could be classified as absolute instrument is...

A] milli ammeter

B] micro ammeter

C] galvanometer

D] <u>tangent galvanomer</u>

160] Which of the following methods of damping is commonly used in moving iron instrument?

A] <u>Air damping</u>

B] fluid damping

C] eddy current damping

D] viscosity damping

161] The deflecting torque of a moving iron instrument is directly proportional to the..

A] current

B] <u>square of the current</u>

C] square root of the current

D] voltage

162]Which of the following is used for measuring the medium resistance directly?

A] ammeter

B] <u>megger</u>

C] ohmmeter

D] voltmeter

163] An ohmmeter is used for measuring the...

A] insulation resistance

B] <u>resistance</u>

C] current

D] potential difference

164] Which of the following components is not a part of an ohmmeter?

A] fixed resistor

B] variable resistor

C] <u>capacitor</u>

D] battery

165] In shunt ohmmeter, maximum deflection signifies ..

A] <u>maximum resistance</u>

B] minimum resistance

C] a fault in the megger

D] none of these

166].An unknown DC voltage is to be measured, which measuring range will you select first?

A] 500V

B] 50V

C] 1.5 V

D] 0.5V

167].An unknown direct current of micro ampere rating is to be measured, which measuring range will you select first?

A] 20 micro amp

B] 15 micro amp

C] 150 micro amp

D] 500 micro amp

168] A multimeter cannot measure...

A] current

B] potential difference

C] capacitance

D] resistance

169] Dynamometer type meters are used to measure...

A] only AC quantities

B] only DC quantities

C] both AC and DC

D] pulsating AC only

170] Which effect is used in wattmeter?

A] electrodynamic effect

B] thermal effect

C] chemical effect

D] electrostatic effect

171] Which of the instrument listed below operates efficiently as wattmeter in both AC and DC?

A] PMMC instrument

B] dynamometer instrument

C] hot wire instrument

D] MI instrument

172] Electrodynamic type of instrument are used commonly for the measurement of...

A] voltage

B] current

C] resistance D]

173] When the phase and neutral of the energy meter are interchanged, its disc...

A] <u>rotates in reverse direction</u>

B] rotates in correct direction

C] will stop

D] rotates slowly

E] rotates at high speed

174] When the disc of energy meter is rotating even without connecting any load, the error is called

A] <u>creeping error</u>

B] phase error

C] friction error

D] temperature error

175] AC single phase energy meters record the energy in the unit of...

A] <u>kilowatt hours</u>

B] number of thousands of disc rotation

C] volt amperes

D] kilo volt ampere

176] A megger measures resistance in...

A] ohms

B] hundreds of ohms

C] thousands of ohms

D] <u>millions of ohms</u>

177] A megger is exclusively designed for measuring..

A] <u>very high resistance</u>

B] very low resistance

C] ground faults in power lines

D] over loads on DC motors

178] For pipe earthing the minimum internal diameter of galvanized iron of steel pipe required is...

A] <u>12.5 mm</u>

B] 16mm

C] 3.5 mm

D] 4 m

179] The earth conductor provides a path to ground for..

A] <u>leakage current</u>

B] over current

C] high voltage

D] circuit current

180] if the size of the circuit copper conductor is 10 sq-mm then the size of earth conductor in G.I] wire should be...

A] 1.5 sq.mm

B] 2.5 sq.mm

C] 5 sq.mm

D] 10 sq.mm

181] One calory is equal to,,,

A] 4187 joules

B] 418.7 joules

C] 41.87 joules

D] 4.187 joules

182] The operating temperature range of electrical stove with bare heating element is...

A] 300◦ to 400◦C

B] 500◦ to 600◦C

C] 550◦ to 900◦C

D] 1100◦ to 1300◦C

183] Which appliance works on heating effect of electric current?

A] incandescent lamp

B] bimetallic thermostat

C] H R C fuse

D] toaster

184] What is the size of nichrome wire for heating element of 1000 watts, 230V heater at 500◦C?

A] 18 SWG

B] 20SWG

C] 24 SWG

D] 25 SWG

185] The heat proof insulating material used for heater base is...

A] mica

B] porcelain

C] asbestos

D] glass wool

186].The temperature regulating component of an automatic electric iron is...

A] heating element

B] thermostat

C] sole plate

D] pressure plate

187].The bread toasting zone temperature is about...

A] 400◦C

B] 800◦C

C] 260◦C

D] 975◦C

188] If a winding makes electrical contact with the metal case of the mixer motor the winding is...

A] grounded

B] open circuited

C] short circuited

D] loose connected

189] If the end shafts of a rotor turns blue it is an indication of...

A] scoring

B] overheating

C] freezing

D] burring

190] What type of motor is used in a food mixer?

A] DC shunt motor

B] universal motor

C] capacitor start motor

D] capacitor start and run motor

191] In what position is the motor mounted in most of the mixers?

A] vertical

B] horizontal

C] inclined

D] parallel

www.ingramcontent.com/pod-product-compliance
Ingram Content Group UK Ltd.
Pitfield, Milton Keynes, MK11 3LW, UK
UKHW021922190726
13853UKWH00002B/796